Peter McDonald was born in Belfast in 1962, and was educated at Methodist College Belfast. He has held teaching positions at the Universities of Cambridge and Bristol, and since 1999 he has been Christopher Tower Student in Poetry in the English Language at Christ Church, Oxford, where he is also Professor of British and Irish Poetry. He is well-known as a poetry critic, and has published four books about verse from the nineteenth and twentieth centuries, as well as an edition of the poetry of Louis MacNeice. He lives with his family in Oxfordshire, and he is working on W. B. Yeats's *Complete Poems* for the Longman Poets series.

Herne the Hunter

PETER McDONALD

CARCANET

First published in Great Britain in 2016 by Carcanet Press
Limited Alliance House, 30 Cross Street, Manchester, M2 7AQ
www.carcanet.co.uk

Typeset by LA in Arnhem Pro & Freight Pro. A CIP catalogue record for
this book is available from the British Library, ISBN 9781784101725.

The publisher acknowledges financial assistance from
Arts Council England.

FSC
www.fsc.org

MIX
Paper from
responsible sources
FSC® C014540

Supported using public funding by
ARTS COUNCIL
ENGLAND

CONTENTS

There is an old tale goes, that *Herne* the Hunter
(Sometime a keeper here in Windsor Forrest)
Doth all the winter time, at still midnight
Walke roundabout an Oake, with great rag'd-hornes,
And there he blasts the tree, and takes the cattle,
And makes milch-kine yeeld blood, and shakes a chaine
In a most hideous and dreadfull manner.
You haue heard of such a Spirit, and well you know
The superstitious idle-headed-Eld
Receiu'd, and did deliuer to our age
This tale of *Herne* the Hunter, for a truth.

(*The Merry Wives of Windsor*, IV, iv)

I

TWO SALMON

I met your beloved in Russell Square, and she was weeping.

Their dead weights balance him: suspending one
on either side, he carries down the fish
he must have killed out on the salmon-run
here where the river slows to water-wash
and salt, and a lazy tide, so in the sun
they glitter from a distance, and they flash
like things that could be animate and raw,
each with its whole weight taken on the jaw.

Two salmon, closer up, and not alive
in their suits of miraculous chainmail
fitted like skin; not enough to survive
out in the parched and dazzling, unreal
element of noise and wind; they arrive
with blood-flecks on the white and pewter scales
along their bellies, each one the same size,
these fish with their uncloseable dead eyes.

I nod to him, smile: it's as if what swings
so heavily from each arm were a new
option, a way of going about things;
for a moment anyhow, the fish are two
lives, and he has his choice of them; he brings
one and the other steadily into
the world with its drizzle of light, its poles
upright between sandbanks and sea. Two souls.

I look and look: eventually, he's gone;
and maybe all of this was wrong, in fact:
remember how two bodies can have one
soul between them, with that soul intact
through all the very worst that can be done
or said; they swim against a cataract

over and over, light sheathing them from above,
two bodies with one single life to prove.

Know all the worst, and see the worst thing whole:
one life neglected by you or betrayed
somewhere beyond its own help or control,
exposed and shivering and all afraid;
walk in the streets, and see a crying soul
that once this body and another made;
look at it without sympathy or surprise;
look at it with your sore, wide-open eyes.

You, meaning me. Because of my own dread
of open gills, fish-scales, and the lithe shine
over packed muscle when it's dried and dead,
the salmon and the fisherman combine
remorselessly in my remorseful head
to plead and punish; again and again
they find me, and I find them, when we go
looking and looking. There is nothing to know.

THE DOWNPOUR

It was too far to run; we gave up running,
and walked together in the thunderstorm
with heads exposed, and our hair raked with hail,
a half-mile back to the room, its made bed
and its roof that moaned and sang with the downpour
going on half the day. We made turbans
out of towels, and lay down on clean sheets
not ours, with furies beating at the door
and only our silence to hold them off:
if we spoke, we said scarcely anything.
Rain hammered on the glass like misery
until we slept, wrapped in our own bare arms.

The wiper that he fixed with chewing-gum
one wet night on his way back from Tyrone
was working well enough to clear the windscreen
     as my father drove my mother home
     across dark hill-roads from the dance;
        his Austin van
       shone headlights into dense
      and shifting waves of drizzle, where
the road rolled down, and up and down, to gleam
every so often with the increasing glare
of another car approaching on full beam.

One such was on a steep hill dead ahead,
in and out through the layers of half-rain
at a fair lick, until it sank right down
      to where the lines of headlamps, payed
      out forwards, would be baffled by
        that drop again
       as the road suddenly
      dipped, and it ducked then out of sight
for a second or two: but what should have led
that car back into view, back to the night,
had failed, and there was empty road instead.

There were no lanes, no places to pull in,
no ditches, or low over-hanging trees;
my mother with her handbag on her knees
      looked quickly to both sides, in vain,
      for a car that, only moments back,
        was about to rise
       out of the dip, on track
      for passing by: no car, and yet
it was there, certainly – a puzzled grin
from my father said as much, as they both sat
watching the moving road and vacant rain.

They thought no more of it, till later on
when my father paid his usual salesman's call
to a farm that lay just over from that hill:
      there was no business to be done,
      for it turned out that very week
        just at nightfall,
        with his hands still on the rake,
      the old farmer who owned the place
and had worked the fields all day, sat himself down
and died: the shock, they said, was still on his face,
nearly a smile, though he'd been there on his own.

SOUNDPROOF

London so noisy that you couldn't hear
the noise – air-brakes and engines, fast alarms
that whooped and stopped, and started up again
while the cars snored, with motor-scooters gunning
a way through them to suddenly take off,
rasping: all of it lost on you and me,
with little any kind of sound could bring
we didn't know, or hadn't heard before,
able to touch each other then through frail
quietly folding layers that enclosed
everything still pristine in its form,
past crowds of strangers on forgotten streets.

Decades ago, I met the crying man
approaching on a pavement steep uphill,
far from wherever all the grief began,

so fast there was no chance for me to plan
another route than where I walked until,
decades ago, I met the crying man

when sycamore leaves, crumpled fan on fan,
ran quick as water through a rumbling mill
far from wherever all the grief began

on speckled stone his wet eyes tried to scan
past blocking tears he couldn't stop or still:
decades ago, I met the crying man

and see him now, as he does all he can
to keep the sobs from flooding him, to kill
far from wherever all the grief began

this man crying; I think I almost ran
to escape his angry tears, their seep and spill.
Decades ago, I met the crying man,
far from wherever all the grief began.

A STING

How delicately, with the breath drawn in,
and the eyes working from so far above
unsteady fingers that they seem to be
helpless and panicked, I must draw the sting
out totally, as a blackbird draws a worm
up from the ground with a sharp grip, stunning
it out of darkness as it turns and squirms;
how definitely I must go ahead,
hurting myself with such needling patience,
if ever I manage to wish back all
the happiness I took, if ever I
draw out the pain this smarting skin completes.

THE NAMES

You knew them by sight,
but when you addressed
invoices all night
to farmers at rest

in the dark out of town,
it was always the same
words you put down
for each farmer's name:

one name would be passed
from father to son;
the first and the last
made two men one,

and the names of the fields
were the names of the men;
like rent and yields
or distances then

all known, if you knew
such things, as you did.
When a breeze came through
and my papers slid

just now, all across
each other – a mess
of writing to toss
in the bin – my address

on tickets, prescriptions,
adverts, bills,
dates for receptions,
cartons of pills,

has you at its head,
where a name that was yours
does duty instead
for mine, and endures

officially now
in a desert of strangers.
Although I allow
advantages, dangers,

all to accrue
as if to some man
I don't know, it's you;
and where I began

is where I end up:
thin pages scattered,
a blown envelope,
with all that mattered

gone in a hurry –
how little I save;
how lightly I carry
your name to the grave.

THE DISTANCE

The power to hurt, not easy to restrain,
that had the power to comfort quietly
those years ago, in all its easy forms,
us half-asleep, exhausted, and our once-
voluble tongues; the little hint of cunning
when silence could mean one or another thing,
and herald such advances and retreats
as lovers make: the power of making terms
with sadness, when no pain is undisclosed,
tries its mute strength now with a noiseless tread
behind me, keeping striking distance, if
I look up, and expect to see you here.

THE PLEIADES

                    If at that time of year
when the weather often comes over as clear
enough to tempt you to set sail, but when
the seven Pleiades, all on the run
from Orion's strength, fall into the dark sea,
then winds and storms can suddenly burst free;
so you are well-advised to keep your boat
out of the water, and to take good note
of me, and work the land.

(Hesiod, *Works and Days,* lines 618–623)

A BIG STICK

Eventually, they all became fair
game for him, the girls with their blown hair

at café tables, on steps outside
talking together, ready to glide

away and glide apart in a breeze
of sunny cold autumn air; and these

were only some of them: others went
further, but he was still on their scent,

tracing them to safe places – not that
safe, as it would turn out. His own flat

was filled with trophies, but it was bare
apart from those: he was never there.

Things stayed on the right side of correct:
no violence, though he never checked;

only disappointment of a kind
in the last looks that needed a blind

eye turned to them. Now October sun
dazzled him, and he saw every one

of them when he laughed about the trick
– *You couldn't beat it with a big stick* –

with light behind them, colder than life,
apart from the busy places, rife

with voices, clatter, buses and cars,
all their faces setting like the stars.

THE LANDSCAPE

Often I discover us spending time
in a low house built very near the shore,
not really hearing noises from the sea
that fill each room, or catching the slow beat
of waves all night, all day; and when a storm
blasts in, sending its long clouds running
over our roof, when the main force of a gale
tries to dislodge us, there we both remain
unmoved, not moving, probably in love
and not a word between us, noticing
light stretch again along the coast ahead
where sandhills turn to lanes and to small farms.

A STORM

What else is there to say? Even this wind
cutting the channel water into lines
of shiny lead and pewter, black and grey,
when it bites your cheek can barely leave behind
a sting; nothing can hurt you, and the signs
blown sideways and blown back, that point awry
to places inland, point to nowhere now
as hoardings crumple down, and power-lines bow.

The weather is the news, and like the news
it has no meaning, nothing to convey
except itself – a lifetime to learn that.
Rain can't decide to fall; the winds don't choose
to turn and face you, facing them today
where your body is part-hidden and pressed flat
against a seawall; now that you stand still,
you feel the soundless vacuum of will

inside this crash and bellow of cold air,
fetching you where little is left to say
except that no one meant this – no one did,
and there's no loss in it, or need to care.
Without either excitement or dismay,
as though it foamed from under the earth's lid,
sea water washes through built-over land
where nobody today would choose to stand.

This is what's left when there is nothing left:
there is no consequence, no price to pay,
seeing how strength breaks up as the storm breaks,
how you are neither fulfilled nor bereft,
how everyone you loved just goes away,
how it all goes away, as the air shakes
with indifferent force, and again the sky
barrels its dark-lit clouds from low to high.

You know this, but you know it by the feel
of hollowness inside your head, the play
of wind and sand and water at your feet,
for what you know is nothing: as a wheel
runs free to nowhere, as there is no stay
against the speed of hail and melting sleet,
you fly with wreckage that the storm has hurled,
and you love nobody in the whole world.

Ice in a swivelled glass
coats itself in vermouth;
the colder evenings pass,
and stars over the roof
back away to a mild
dome in the distance, as
each one is ranged and filed
by quadrant, azimuth.

The ice-cubes snick and clunk:
behind us, a cliff face;
ahead, pale and part-sunk
in shadow, the last trace
of daytime on broad streets
recedes, where traffic's race
is a bright line that repeats
itself to bound this place.

If stars figure the truth,
it's one that we can't read;
in between lip and tooth,
ice numbs whatever need
there is to make my mouth
say what has to be said
long past the end of youth:
a good or a bad deed.

THE DROP

I had the sense that it was very near
and yet might be kept far away by shunning
anything like an opportunity
to bring the edge another step closer
or actually look, see the drop plain
at my feet, then choose whether to cling
by standing where I was, or not. The chance
is always there, a chill that nothing warms,
bellowing, empty, never to be closed
or covered up with silence and pure dread,
unknowable, where what is chosen meets
what has to happen, with no choice at all.

HERNE THE HUNTER

1

With everything wrong, no right way to behave –
even so, this was the worst I could devise:
brutal, when it might have been otherwise.
Are you supposed to take that to the grave?

Once you can bear to look, you see a grove
of elm and ash, where great gashes, the size
of open fists are cut, and the bark lies
in strips and ribbons everywhere:
                                    to save
anything now from all the fury and pain
seems barely possible, and such unmeant
gouging and shredding, more or less insane,
that made this carnage just to find some ease
is no worse than we knew, watching the trees
stand still to take their unjust punishment.

2

Is it alive, or not? It is alive,
but threadbare and scooped-looking now, for all
that it succeeds in standing proud and tall,
this cedar, whose old upper boughs contrive
nest-platforms when the building birds arrive,
but not today: today, when a wet squall
strikes the poor man up there, and makes him fall
down through the brittle wood in a high dive.

Is he dead on impact, cut raw, or lamed
when he smacks the forest floor like a bag of bones?
We cannot know, because he never lands,
having slipped long since from the tree's hands,
and stepped out of the air to soil and stones
where the stricken cedar is, tall and ashamed.

3

In the end, there was nothing that I denied;
spelling out guilt like a bad alphabet
in fear, without remorse, I simply let
words lose themselves in the quick tears I cried.

To tap a pine, you cut into its side
through bark and into flesh, into the wet
flesh, where now little v-shapes are set
like signs, carved neatly from narrow to wide
all round the trunk; and there, to catch the new
resin, plastic half-cups and trays are taped.

It comes so slowly you don't see it come
at first, the sticky gradual pine-gum,
like blood that drops and hardens once it's tapped,
or downward-crawling tears that you see through.

4

She stood above him on the moving stairs
and looked around, and smiled, and held his gaze
so that time seemed to stop, go out of phase
with life before and after: unawares,
he stepped up to a height of flashes, flares,
split-second beacons whose strength could amaze
them both together, and leave them in a daze,
pale at a whole world so suddenly theirs.

This was the fullness of a chestnut tree
bursting with lights, dwarfing the two of them;
its blossoms the same colour as the silk
against her skin; its breath enormous, free;
each thousandth leaf held fast on a new stem:
next day, the cows gave blood instead of milk.

5

The trees take shape, and blur their shapes in spring
with white and pink, as random shots of bloom
come everywhere at once with flounce and plume
of excess show, puffing a bright ring
out in a rising circle, that can bring
its fuzzy glare to dead space, fill a room
with erotic, all-imaginary perfume:
the cherry- and the plum-trees blossoming.

Love-poets ought to write with a quill pen
for her alone, or readers in close pairs,
and not for blowsy sorrows of their own;
May gives a tree more light than the tree bears,
unpicking it until the flowers are blown,
while lovers hasten seriously upstairs.

6

From this distance, the birch saplings engrave
thin lines of grey on lighter grey, embrace
each other, tangle, and so interlace
their own likenesses, where they seem to wave
stiffly in the wind.

          Today, when I shave,
I watch my face become my father's face:
he was the better man.

          Whatever trace
there is – if there is anything left, save
these low trees, far away and vulnerable –
to stand in for first things, a few half-bright
resemblances, glowing, ready to pall,
that come and go into and out of sight,
will figure there, just about visible
as birch-bark mirrors the blank early light.

7

Hawthorn to heal the heart: beneath an arc
of blossom, fizzing as it jumps and jigs
with every gust, how many jaggy sprigs
would you need to cut away from leaves and bark
for that medicine to work?

                                    I see a mark
on each leg, where the sharp cord snaps and digs
at your skin, and lines etched there like twigs
that touch each other gently in the dark.

Thorn runs under the tiny flowers, and faces
upwards beneath them, where you wouldn't see
as you close a hand, then in a dozen places
it leaves its little wounds, intricately
arranged in salmon-and-black corsetry
with hooks and eyes, and buttons and tight laces.

8

And sometimes real tears without warning come,
as if grief could please itself, and these dry
eyes could not take in the tan-yellowy
hazel switches across them without some
working of sudden sorrow, sorrow dumb
about its reasons, but still tuning a cry
past hearing, and pitching itself so high
that leaves and bending wood vibrate and thrum.

I am speaking with the accents of the dead
– my dead, I mean – whose voices are entwined
with mine, and break apart inside my head
then fade to almost nothing here, behind
my speech and breath when, just over what's said,
I hear a cry of spirits, faint and blind.

9

This last knock split it open, the maple wood
solid until it's broken, only then
coming apart slowly along the grain,
not as strong as it's heavy, and though good
for many things, not for this.
                              Whatever should
have happened, didn't: ten or a dozen men
couldn't budge me, get me loose, or unpen
me from the narrow cage in which I stood.

That strength was weakness really: a mistake
to leave the timber just as it was found
and try to use it, then to watch it break
as it must – as the maples all around
would break in the end, having to forsake
their inward fibres, hard and seldom sound.

The patch of mud and moss we called the green,
where footballs whacked and skidded half the day
from children sent out of the house to play,
had three young beeches, each behind a screen
of staked wire netting: as we ran between
them, frantic, we would pull the wire away
on each sharp turn, making them jerk and sway
to kicks and pulls, letting them drag and lean.

Too damaged over months, the trees gave up,
their short lives hurt past bearing. Nothing brings
them back, not even this; and not the look
of them dying, the look of broken things;
but noise after them carried, didn't stop:
frail cages sounded like chains as they shook.

Rain-water and the water from the stream
coat shelves of stone, where willow-shadows break
up into abstract cuts of light and dark
the greys and green-greys: nothing is the same
for more than seconds, as the waters teem
down and across and down.

                    All for the sake
of love – really – its well sewn-in mistake
ripped out, a stitched heart torn along the seam;
all for just that, and the threads brushed away.

I can't make out a pattern. Where they sway
with higher winds, the willow branches tilt
downwards and tangle, disordered in the pelt
of rain, and each leaf twists a different way
across limestone that water wants to melt.

I kept on seeing the very same oak tree
blasted; sometimes in dreams; sometimes I saw
it really, worried and ragged and raw,
when I had to picture it incessantly
not to see other things, and not to be
taken apart myself, as though the paw
of some black beast had put claw after claw
onto my skin, opened me as a key
opens a lock.

       And what there was to find
was only this: a mess of nerves and blood;
flesh that was going to die anyway
rooted in soil and loam, gravel and mud;
in love doubtless with what it leaves behind;
not saying to the end what it would never say.

AT BUSHFOOT

This current speeding up and shallowing
closer and closer to the flattened sand
– the big waves there, and killing cross-currents –
splashes around your ankles as you stand
right at the edge of its tan-coloured water
where the Bush river stops being a river
and splays into the ocean like a hand.

Faster and nearer as it rides the pebbles,
quicker and colder, coming to its end,
river-water turns over and keeps turning
over everything that daylight can send,
changing by yards the faint, peat-tinted
stain of land for fast-cutting reflections
of the sky in its wobbly rush and blend.

The dogs, who just can't keep themselves from jumping
in and wading here, bark against the wind
as their owners talk and look away, still talking;
but you keep quiet where these waves rescind
the river's flow, holding and pushing it sideways,
drawing the colour out, while they sound over
a stony course where the currents are twinned.

Two kinds of water are one kind of water,
one thing forever becoming some other thing;
for this is what you see as you look downwards,
and your life moves beneath you, quickening
with the earth's light and with the light of heaven
that pull and tumble across one another
while shifting stones at your feet click and ring.

ANTS

Late daylight was the only thing that raked
them, spoil-heaps of downfallen larch-leaves;
and but for these the flattened field was naked,
though thin-stripped branches made a kind of arch
above our heads as we walked underneath them
not looking up, or back, but looking outwards
onto a bellowing and sky-wide heath,
no match for each other: I thought about
how sun made all the puddles into tinfoil,
lighting the worlds we walked over by chance
and tiny lives everywhere near the soil;
about the ants I powdered in their death-dance –
frantic for life and crazy with the toxin,
finishing before they could well begin.

THE SWORDS

Each out of its embroidered sheath,
flat in the case and bright beneath
two tiny spotlamps at a tilt,
one sword points at another's hilt,
a thin moon against a thin moon
showing clear in the sky at noon,
except this room is dark and there's
no sky, where many swords in pairs
point at each other in the light
which only just fills those airtight
plush spaces inside which they shine
and never move: these two align
themselves, as the occasion serves,
on open and enclosing curves.

They might be parts of a circle which
will never close here, as they pitch
in an arrested sweep of force
that zooms to sever or divorce
one thing from any other thing
it cuts across, that breaks the ring
its own shape is a part of; now
they neither allow nor disallow
the fearful step, the sure defeat,
like two lovers who dare not meet
ever again, so terrible
the strength between them when they pull
into each other's range, or start
to feel themselves drawing apart.

And terrible is not the word:
turn a deaf ear to such absurd
efforts to state the awful thing,
the truth without its clinching ring
which you can almost hear sound out

behind that rough and sudden shout
of anger riven with sheer grief
coming, predictable and brief,
to break in two your every night –
no word for that is ever right,
yet could be caught somewhere between
two pointing blades with their worked sheen;
steel isn't pure, but the pure steel
divides all you can speak and feel.

Outside, the sky is full of flakes
where falling cherry-blossom makes
hanami-clouds above the heads
of picnickers on dry grass beds,
the flasks and paper cups, the neat
parcels of shopping at their feet,
and blows across the paths across
the park, bunches like candy-floss
at each corner, sweet-softening
the hard edges of everything,
to shuffle up in weightless drifts
that even a weak breeze soon lifts,
as crowds move slowly through, and go
in between flower-lights, high and low.

But you are in this room alone:
for minutes now, your eyes have grown
used to the nearly-dark, and so
fixed on the cases' low-power glow
that all they see is pair on pair
of swords contained in dustless air
as if vision were sharp and hard,
tempered, and never off its guard,
cutting straight through the things it sees
with looks like blades, and blades like these;
yet even as it holds its ground
such eyesight turns itself around,
swivelling the held force within
to try an edge against your skin.

Force seems to cancel force, but no:
force locks on force, and they both go
pushing into each other, long
past any stage of being strong;
a stillness ready to explode
from weaknesses that never showed
in centuries, but might be there,
impossible to see or bear.
Two swords in a whole room of swords,
displayed so that they point towards
each other beneath air and glass
don't move, yet still won't let you pass
now that you want to be away;
older than you, but here to stay.

II

In from the Cregagh Road, through the showroom,
its rolled Axminster and new Parker Knoll,
full of himself and beaming like a bridegroom
up the aisle, with a whiskey pitch and roll
back from the pub, straight into the lit gloom
of my mother's back-office cubby-hole
walked Leahy, brandishing like contraband
two pheasants that he swung from either hand.

A cock-pheasant and hen-pheasant, each one
with its neck stretched down from a tiny head
and its body barely ruffled from the gun;
the male's green balaclava splashed with red
around each eye, and long feathers half done-
up and half undone where the wing-tips spread;
the female with her dead shape duller brown
and buxom, a barred tail stiff and pointed down.

Leahy's big frame blocked the whole office door
when he came on in proudly with the brace
of birds, all mischief and jovial uproar,
dangling their bodies in my mother's face
with 'There you are, ye girl!', ready to pour
them both into her lap, and take his place
as the bringer-in of luxury and delight
or some abundant spirit of the night.

His own body weighed down and flushed, one bead
of sweat on the red brow, its hot flesh tones
glowing in from the cold, he took the lead
that evening between ledgers and telephones
because he had to, or the simple need
aching and echoing in hollow bones
made him; or his good nature; or the rife
sorrows and wants that filled this part of life.

High spirits and abiding anguish, time
passing through blood as it forces a rift
between the soul and flesh – his stratagem,
if it was that, his spur-of-the-moment gift
was doomed: 'Two birds,' she sobbed at home, 'and them
with the heads and feathers still on them': she'd lift
her fearful face to look me in the eye:
'Dead birds – but why would Leahy do that? Why?'

He hadn't known how much she was afraid
of feathered things, until he saw her tears
that night, the angry panic as she made
her exit past him, speechless, through the chairs
and sofas, rugs and tables where he stayed
alone – poor Robert Leahy, dead these years,
the life in him so strong, but even then
heavy between the cock-pheasant and hen.

Caught by the foot in a toothed trap
– a loaded, unsprung clink and snap
from the nowhere in which it lay –
this hare will never lope away
again, and starts its awful, plain
work now through a blaze of pain
on the one thing that's to be done,
as though by maiming it could run
itself back from the dreadful place
where its choice is whether to face
death certainly, or the chance of death:
it lives on, breath by minute breath,
until its strength or the bone gives,
just for however long it lives.

A COACH AND HORSES

As though his head wasn't away entirely
when he drove the old man round, night in, night out;
as though he'd any notion, or the least doubt
     whether he came late or came early
     wherever he arrived or left,
       or was about
     when both of them would drift
     in through gates that might well be closed
against them, closed and bound and fastened squarely;
many a time Dulligan almost dozed
at the wheel, but for the boss's push and shout.

If he knew the roads at all, it was by feel:
their gradients and surfaces combined
somehow were just enough for him to find
     the place to slow, or turn the wheel,
     and keep himself out of the ditch,
      taking a blind
     corner without a hitch
     on mizzly evenings when he drove
a coach and horses through the iron or steel
between him and wherever he'd arrive,
between the road before him and behind.

Not everyone had seen him, even though
plenty had heard about some start-and-stall
chaotic lurch into a hedge or wall
     that should have laid Dulligan low,
     and knew how he would drive at night,
      a head-the-ball
     safest when out of sight
     and out of mind completely; few
wanted to meet him going fast or slow,
whatever townland they were driving through,
and wanted to see his boss the least of all.

A shape might come towards you, then be gone
nowhere, and there'd be only the leaves blowing
around upwards in front of you, and showing
      nothing but the air they rode on;
      like a closed box coming unshut,
        all the time growing,
         and then him with his head cut
      driving it, not able to look
where he was rushing, the same Dulligan
who could vanish in a blink, but always took
the same road from wherever he was going.

SNIPE

As the wetland lays itself bare,
clouds blurring water into air
at seventy or sixty yards
are far from his only safeguards:
barely visible when he's down
in his suit of streaked buff and brown,
the snipe's idea of a straight flight
sends him off to the left or right
at random, and from high to low
going to where he wants to go.
On a fool's errand, pointlessly
shuffling through weeds so as to see
better, levelling over again,
a first-time shot curses the rain.

The thing you need to hear, I cannot say:
addled and tongue-tied, never more than when
faces come close to mine, and go away

into the roaring light of their own day;
to your face, or with the flourish of a pen,
the thing you need to hear, I cannot say.

A wind at gale force bundles to the bay
my own voice with black clouds, and though again
faces come close to mine, and go away,

your face among them, I would still delay
telling the truths you have from other men:
the thing you need to hear, I cannot say.

Not reticence: a familiar display
unfair and desperate; if nine or ten
faces come close to mine, and go away,

I owe more than lament and poor dismay
to them, I owe the truth; but even then
the thing you need to hear, I cannot say:
faces come close to mine, and go away.

BOAR

No matter which way the wind blows,
he knows the smell of you, he knows
you're there; and keeping far enough
apart to suit him, where the rough
wood-edge and sloping briar-bank,
wet leafmould slippery and rank
with leaves of garlic rotting down
from olive-yellow to black-brown
surrounds you, as it surrounds him:
now the rain drenches flank and limb
alike, you hear him shunt and snort
deep into something that falls short
of what his stubby tusks and snout
can scent or fathom or prise out.

Something makes me say it all happened near
borderlands in south Fermanagh, or else
right at the edge of Monaghan and Tyrone;
more certainly, this was the fifties, when he
made visits every six or seven weeks
taking orders, and dropping off items for Jack
up and down the country (for the NORTHERN
WHOLESALE STORES, that is, JOHN GRAHAM PROP.,
GOVERNMENT SURPLUS, SADDLES, LEATHER AND IRON
MERCHANTS, 25 UNIVERSITY ROAD,
BELFAST), so customers knew him by sight,
kept him talking, and talked plenty to him,
over big mugs of tea, when the most
they got back was his plain 'Do you tell
me that?', smiling, half-earnest, and then
laughter, small business, and off on his way.

She was married to one sullen and coarse
old farmer, who gave her a terrible life
('*coorse*', he'd say, making fun of the voice).
Each time he visited, she would come out
dressed for town, but stand talking instead
seriously to him, all about how
she was treated there like one of the beasts:
would he maybe bring her something the next
time, for she wasn't let past the gate?
Fifty Gallaher's Blues, for preference. So
that's what he did – and where was the harm? –
fetching her supplies for the most of a year,
every time hearing more from her, till the day
she asked straight out, full-face, 'Will you take
me back with you, away the hell out of here?
It's you, or the next man that comes to this door.'

Everybody in this story is dead.
I can see the look he gave her, the pretence
this was all a joke; hear him saying goodbye,
making light of the whole thing: but a few
weeks afterwards, always regular, back
he came, the usual gift tucked in his hand,
to find her away – away, he was told,
with the gypsies. The truth of it was
she had really gone, she never returned
though he did, on schedule, month after month.
She was too young to stay, and he was
too young to be stupid; the two of them were
far too young, lost in the land of the young,
where people are always just going away.
For years he looked out for her, and still
kept spare packs of cigarettes in the van.

A little squeal, and then the sound
of a spring being tightly wound
in on itself, is all there is
at first, a sudden note and whizz-
whirr coming from the bunched-up grass;
but maybe as the minutes pass
and you lie still, you start to see
a round bird moving clumsily,
all body, getting ready now
to risk the air, and chance a low
flight that will take it further out
from the covey: as if in doubt,
and happier with the ground below,
it hesitates; it doesn't go.

THE CLUB

I saw great Orion too,
herding the spirits of the beasts he slew
on earth, where they had lived apart from men
on the abandoned mountains, and now again
grazed in a field of asphodel: his hands
still held that club, weighted and wrapped with bands
of metal, and hard forever.

(*Odyssey,* book XI, lines 572–5)

When he counted them, he had run through
fifty, there were fifty of them, who

lay on the ground for him, who lay down
under him; then when the grass was brown

and burnt at the end of summer, he
tracked the setting stars for company

and thought of the payback for all this,
the dawn after dawn that he would miss,

away in the dark, touching thin air;
a field, and the big gates broken there,

beasts escaping he would never catch,
with the clumsiest more than a match

for him: all of it coming soon now,
and he could do nothing but allow

the seven sisters to rise and set
in colder winds, and with the ground wet

beneath them where they sank. So he would
be blind; nothing might do any good

except to follow where he was led,
fixing his two useless eyes ahead

and standing before those walls of light
where all his lovers now rose upright

facing him, starting to make him feel
his years, and daring the eyes to heal.

MALLARD

Face-down from a green-shiny hood,
as targets go he cuts a good
figure among the reeds and deep
willow-litter; wet, half-asleep,
like the slow bird he came to shoot.
Between a tree-trunk and dead root,
not caring now if he leaves traces,
dullard, he leans back and braces
everything, although there's no point,
into that aching shoulder-joint
while the mallard float-dips away
past his aim and its disarray.
There's not a sound, or hint of a sound,
as he turns the fowling-piece around.

SEA DEER

At this distance, with sight like mine, there could
be either one or two animal-shapes
moving a little on the further dunes:
on four legs, certainly; looking for food
among those tangled sand-grasses perhaps,
when the summer wind blows up, and attunes
bushes and wiry hedges to one low
far-back repeating chord, quiet and slow.

My own slow pace is in and out of waves,
a fat man in his bathing-trunks, alone,
wading through bladderwrack close to the shore,
who has to squint against the light he braves
to see where everybody else has gone;
if this is a landscape, I belong no more
than do these two dark and improbably
heraldic creatures that I think I see.

The ragged outline of one distant head
might be its horns, or antlers – how could deer
come out this far? But even so, the calm
outlines are the size of deer, somehow led
to where the land gives up, with the sea near
and never stopping. Antlers, yes, each palm
and beam on which the tiny moving lines
are brow and bay, surroyal and royal tines.

Two beasts that seem to wobble and return
where my eyelashes brush their silhouettes:
bearing the details I have never seen,
they brandish themselves, making me unlearn
the forks and branches that a life forgets;
they mean this, if their business is to mean,
apart from sand and water, and the sting
of air, the cold unintent of everything.

In different elements, we keep away
from one another: both of them, if there
are two, stay at some absolute remove.
A minute more, and yet I couldn't say
what's walking, or stands still; now, as my bare
skin shivers in the breeze, I cannot prove
the two of them are there, or that they've gone,
or even tell the true from the false one.

THE TABLE

An empty plate of stone
cools nothing more than air,
its purpose only one
damaged beyond repair,
as cells by the million
invisibly expire,
not to be back again
exactly as they were.

Nobody comes to say
what to be ready for;
what good it does to play
brave, and to shut the door
thinking we have the way
to make its hinges stir;
hearts we broke in a day
broken for evermore.

What was done on the spur
proves to be done for good,
and I cannot prepare
a shadowy ghost food,
spreading leaves everywhere
and scattering out crude
mosses like scraps of fur
over blunt shreds of wood.

High up in the dead cedar, someone has carved
a figure of Jesus stretched over the cross:
his polished face, angular and half-starved,
faces downwards, like that of a man diving
in free-fall to the ground, ready to toss
his life away, and then see death arriving
bang on time, almost already there,
upwards towards him through breathtaking air.

What god would ever want this for himself?
If once he looked out forwards, he would see
a line of mountains, the snowed-over shelf
of Mount Lebanon, the Kadisha valley
stretched underneath it, and even each tree
around him, adding to the cedar-tally
one – but he looks down, and is looking still
down to the earth with a singular will.

Living a second, discontinuous life,
the tour-guide talks to us about the war,
phalanges, sects, and the contours of strife
that make a map of his imagination;
how close he came, or came at least not far
from death when a hand-grenade's conflagration
caught him out of nowhere, on the left side:
a friend next to him and a stranger died.

He remembers how the air was sucked away
all in an instant, how the blast was not
noise but a silence opening; the spray
of soil and stones and blood together going
in the wrong direction, and a vacuum, hot
and fast, pulling him inwards; a force growing
enormous in a second; then the fear
just after, as they dragged his body clear.

And now the same man stands here fit and whole
below this Jesus of the Maronites,
his talk of trees, and the cedar-patrol
that guards year-round the few of them still standing;
the dangers of dry summers and cold nights,
and names of birds here, flying off or landing
close to their hidden nests somewhere above
all of our heads in the protected grove.

What we might say, standing on his deaf side,
is lost, but he laughs and nods anyway;
how much is spoken, how much more implied
about things by the people who have seen them
hangs like a question, balancing today
in two natures with the one will between them:
even the thin air at this altitude
smells of needles and undecaying wood.

A NIGHT SKY

1

If ever, now; now would be the right time,
when nothing ever after could be worse:
the sky drained, ready for the moon to climb,
with small birds raucous, and the pigeons terse;
if ever a day's heat could end in cold,
and the night-winds bring on a day of rain;
if there was ever a moment to be bold
and face outright the things that are all pain;

if ever, now: but now their strength has gone
from more than the last sunlight and the sky,
courage has little left to settle on,
and all its sounds make one unearthly cry:
there's nothing left, either to join or sever,
make whole or take to pieces now, if ever.

2

Like somebody who sees, or thinks he sees,
past layers of thin cloud in the early night
a new moon rising, I begin to tease
a shape out from the far edge of my sight
and turn it into you, as you might look
apart from life, where reflections slip faint
outlines around a form, maybe the fluke
image of you, with their frail tint and taint.

Much as clouds thicken, sadness makes the lines
blur, lose themselves, fall back, steadily fade
to what could pass for nothing, and outshines
only the shadows solid bodies make:
its half-glow strengthens almost to a blink,
then leaves a ghost-light to recede and sink.

3

Twice every day, cold water in the sea
covers a causeway over rocks and weed,
at low tide walkable and slippery
light-coloured sandstone, three or four feet wide,
up to an unmanned lighthouse just offshore,
a path that comes and vanishes and comes
again in all weathers, a half-sunk floor
between crags where the wind warbles and hums.

Returning regular as day and night,
remorse, isolate, strides down the high road
with cries and calls between distress and spite,
to take whatever payment might be owed:
desire and lack are all it wails and raves;
no respite but the chilly, rising waves.

4

Shy of the daylight, animals unseen
to us work through their decay and their prime;
winter and summer and the months between
turn into each other for the umpteenth time
and still from black-wrapped trees and hidden holes
in earth, the foxes and the owls embark
to search out in their desperate patrols
nightwalking victims, cautious in the dark.

The silence makes me hear things, makes me hear
you, and whatever the sounds you were trying
to pick out, off-key, high as if with fear,
from far off when the spirits you heard crying
were all the hunted creatures, innocent,
gone to their deaths long since, never silent.

5

I know that I should say the better thing
to you, although poor reasons could be tried
to plead a cause, show new bruises, and bring
you for a while to something like my side;
I know exactly what you need to hear
and the hard detail of what's to be told,
final and reeling, as when sun rakes clear
whole fields of stone and brambles in the cold.

And yet I know I needn't tell you this,
for you can see me now, in flat daylight,
like a target impossible to miss
struck over and over in a fair fight:
whoever leaves me sprawling on the floor
will love you better, I know, if not more.

6

Remember that the soul cannot return
and, if it did, would not be welcomed back;
its lightest footsteps, so hard to discern
on the bare roads, and the true sound they lack,
are things the better now for having vanished
into the further stretches of each night
where nothing waits for the weak spirit, banished
to an offshore rock, a long-abandoned light:

it breathes sea-water and breathes cutting wind,
manning a station at the edge of death,
all warmth gone with the blood it left behind,
more distant that lost love, or living breath.
The waves are blacker where the light would fall:
remembering this, you can forget it all.

7

Her turn now to say nothing, turn aside
like a wronged spirit hearing talk in hell
from the lover who betrayed her once and lied,
sorry and voluble to no avail;
her turn to scorn with silence, and rejoin
a past he never asked about, where now
for ever she belongs, and where her pain
is nothing he can disown or allow.

The last he sees of her is her black hair
going into the dark, going too soon;
he can no more reach out and touch her there
than touch a night sky without stars or moon,
no more hear her than listen to the cries
of stones, grievous with their own weight and size.

8

I wanted to dig through topsoil to clay,
knowing there would be nothing, knowing there
would be only the weight as it gave way
under my weight, this ground hard to lay bare;
I wanted to peel back with my own hands
layers that stuck and crumbled, and so toil
away that legs and feet could give commands
against thick stones and dead roots in the soil;

and yet their straining orders went unheeded
until the very shovel seemed to bend,
for all the push to get to what I needed
was pushed against, and wasted in the end:
it was my strength at fault, a never-daunted
courage that ruined all I ever wanted.

9

Not once did I put anything away
for fear of the blunt hurt that it would do;
nothing that I could give back or unsay
did I return or say again to you;
not once did the bright surfaces of things
taken as fragile, intricate, no more,
seem any the less bright for what time brings,
knowing they were all broken at the core;

instead, I kept their brittle pieces close
together, and I watched them, without hope
or pleasure, just watched them, numb and morose,
my face struck by the hard end of a rope
still knotted, whose blind force could lay me flat:
not once, but times past number I did that.

The line between unhappiness and joy,
recrossed so often, was no more a line
than the pen in my hand was only a toy
when it found lies and fantasies to sign
my name to; no more than the line between
imagining and laying down the law,
shading away the truth and coming clean,
between what I saw and I thought I saw:

there was a difference, impossible
to picture or locate; there was a change
somewhere I couldn't name, but I could tell
that it had come, that everything was strange
I'd ever known, all sorrow, yet no more
sorrow than happiness had been before.

The dawn frost like a bloom across flat ground;
jet-trails over the sky like shallow scores;
thorn hedges like wires tangled and unwound;
cars closing on us fast like slamming doors;
the first blow like a hammer to the heart;
the pressure of a hand like taken breath;
cold air like famine, prising lives apart;
long fences broken like the gates of death;

like you and me, the ghosts that walk these lanes;
like winter wind, the blast of memory;
like portraits, the half-icy windowpanes;
like flimsy litter, leaves as they work free:
the future and the past, like drought and dearth,
here dazzle, but like nothing on this earth.

I half expect to meet her coming back
here at the entrance to the cul-de-sac,
though she will scarcely recognise the child
whose look must puzzle her, who never left
this place, still at the door of a red-tiled
hall, and just staring, silently bereft.

This must be when I fall in love with her
in the full light of a drizzly cold day,
on a stone path that's damaged past repair,
its ground never imaginable-away,
where I watch in her eyes only the dark
that must come in between us, both apart,
to bring a night sky without star or spark:
I see the end, even here at the start.

All around us, the daylight has turned green:
far-stretching trees on each side of the river
grow in the wind and on the sun they filter
to make a tattered, hardly-moving screen
above us, where our three faces are shining,
drenched by reflections from the running water
that keeps these big stones slippery and clean.

As though we were all hidden in deep light,
moving at speed and good at keeping quiet,
we might follow the last of the O'Cahans,
their old ghosts still expertly out of sight
like the day-wary, solitary otter
we think we're tracking, always that bit further
away around the next bend, sitting tight.

If we could cross the water with one leap
and then – a dog's leap was it, or a horse's? –
bring word of trouble coming, ward off trouble
in the bright branches and the sap and seep
of tree-roots high above these river pathways,
we would see outright all the scattering creatures
and join them in the silence that they keep.

Over the water, far under the sky,
birds dart away from view on the hunt for insects,
and we can sense that this whole place is teeming
as living things retreat, regroup, slip by;
we are all river-light – look at our faces –
but in the here and now, close to the open
where colours like these brighten as they die.

At last, he's standing at the top
of things, over a scrubby drop
sheer to the river, with its stones
lifted and bared like knuckle-bones;
against spot-lighted brakes and leaves
where he no longer bolts or weaves
away, against their bronze and red,
his flank first, then his hornless head
flares out, and stays utterly still:
you hear him breathing, breathing till
the end, if that's what has to be,
and the living white shape you see
won't run further from what he knows:
right here is as far as it goes.

This winter you read all his letters again,
brought out one by one from the chocolate box
where you let them keep, bundled by the year.
Holding them to the best light you could find,
you tried to make each line come into line,
for now that you see only the edges of things
it takes long work to settle and unbend
words where they ravel and fray, then convert
them to sense, like a scholar in old age
matching the pieces; but you managed it,
helped by remembering what you once read,
now you were reading it for the last time.

Do people write love-letters anymore?
Messages, or whatever it is they send,
short words and tiny pictures gone in flocks
past fetching back, never put on a page,
and harder to remember, aren't the same.
He wrote these words when he was in his prime,
and in the daylight your sore patience brings
his voice home, back from somewhere near the start.
Already you know every word that's said,
for nothing here is new: he's right as rain,
as if he'd see you later in the week,
each time another blurry line comes clear.

And there you are now, where the seagulls' wings
clear out the sky, far up, and the whole shore
is visible, bright as noon, every bit
a real place where he is, and you with him,
the waves so big you have to raise his head
closer to yours before one word is plain,
so loud now that no matter how alert
you are, you might as well resort to mime
to overcome the water's rush and rage.

I needn't ask you what you're doing here,
for this is where everything washes clean
away from your eyes, as they go more blind.

The door is closed where someone knocks and knocks;
they can wait there all morning, you don't mind.
No reason why you shouldn't just remain
here, where the ground is lit up like a stage
for miles, then miles on miles; with a light heart,
so light it's almost weightless, you might hit
the proper name for this wide-open place,
if ever you had named it: the waves pour
over its moving sand that never changes.
In the Irish that neither of us can speak
it is *Tír na nÓg*, the land of youth, and where
nothing goes far, or ever comes to an end.

I see it as if the thin bars of a cage
laid a grid across that sky, and small rain
was changing the light; but it keeps its shine
enough to make my eyes sore. When I hear
you say deliberately, with your voice weak,
how well you loved him, everything arranges
itself for me wherever it might fit:
I loved badly, hurt others, and brought hurt
on my own head – but you couldn't see my face
even if I said so, or if I could send
word of it to your ears, through the great roar
where voices only whisper, and blood sings.

Nobody there knows they've been left behind,
or that we might be looking, listening.
As a gull takes off with something in its beak,
the clouds high up demolish and restore
themselves, raked by the same sun, and the rocks
hold their colours. Now we begin to gauge
everybody's look; the last of the race,
we are the simplest shapes that float and flit

unnoticed at the edge of things, and then
go away from the landmarks and the signs
we knew, and they know, with faces that smart
where a salt-showery breeze picks up, and stings.

Some of the poems in this book appeared first in the following publications, to whose editors I am grateful: *Agenda*, *Archipelago*, *The Edinburgh Review*, *The Irish Times*, *Oxford Poetry*, *Times Literary Supplement*, *The Yellow Nib*. 'The Swords' arises from a visit to Japan made in 2012; I am grateful to my hosts, C. E. J. Simons and the International Christian University, Tokyo.

Two Salmon: This poem is indebted to Seamus Heaney, and is published now in his memory. The epigraph is taken from a note by W. B. Yeats (on his early verse), dated 1925 and first published in 1933: '[...] I saw a man at Rosses Point carrying two salmon. "One man with two souls," I said, and added, "O no, two people with one soul." [...] I remember the mystical painter Horton, whose work had little of his personal charm and real strangeness, writing me these words, "I met your beloved in Russell Square, and she was weeping," by which he meant that he had seen a vision of my neglected soul.'

Herne the Hunter: The last line of sonnet 8 is quoted from Sir Philip Sidney, 'A Farewell' (*Certaine Sonets*):

Oft have I musde, but now at length I finde,
Why those that die, men say they do depart:
Depart, a word so gentle to my minde,
Weakely did seeme to paint deaths ougly dart.
But now the starres with their strange course do binde
Me one to leave, with whome I leave my hart.
I heare a crye of spirits faint and blinde,
That parting thus my chiefest part I part.

Part of my life, the loathed part to me,
Lives to impart my wearie clay some breath.
But that good part, wherein all comforts be,
Now dead, doth shew departure is a death,
Yea worse then death, death parts both woe and joy,
From joy I part still living in annoy.

The final line of sonnet 9 is drawn from Edmund Spenser, *The Faerie Queene*, I–i–9: 'the Maple seldom inward sound'.

Roe: The O'Cahan clan were the rulers of the Limavady area in Co. Derry until 1628. Once, when under siege from the O'Donnels of Donegal, the O'Cahans sent a wolfhound out from their castle to fetch help, which it did by leaping across the river Roe.